YOUR KNOWLEDGE HAS VALUE

Bibliographic information published by the German National Library:

The German National Library lists this publication in the National Bibliography; detailed bibliographic data are available on the Internet at http://dnb.dnb.de .

Imprint:

Copyright © 2015 GRIN Verlag, Open Publishing GmbH
Print and binding: Books on Demand GmbH, Norderstedt Germany
ISBN: 9783656987840

This book at GRIN:

http://www.grin.com/en/e-book/337302/type-2-diabetes-a-comparison-of-the-awareness-in-the-asian-indian-culture

Henriette Frädrich

Type 2 diabetes. A comparison of the awareness in the Asian Indian Culture and the USA

GRIN Publishing

GRIN - Your knowledge has value

Since its foundation in 1998, GRIN has specialized in publishing academic texts by students, college teachers and other academics as e-book and printed book. The website www.grin.com is an ideal platform for presenting term papers, final papers, scientific essays, dissertations and specialist books.

Outline

1. Theoretical and cultural Background 1

   1.1. Main risk factors for developing Type 2 Diabetes..1

   1.2. Awareness of influencing factors for developing and preventing Type 2 Diabetes.................2

   1.3. Awareness and use of alternative medicine for treating Diabetes 2

2. Leading question and presumptions...3

3. Method and corpus 3

4. Approach and results 4

   4.1. Frequency of Type 2 Diabetes in Indian English and U.S. English 4

   4.2. Frequency of overweight and obesity...5

   4.3. Type 2 Diabetes and its correlation with overweight and obesity 5

   4.4. Awareness of different forms of treatment for Type 2 Diabetes 6

5. Summary and discussion...8

6. References 10

1. Theoretical and cultural Background

For some time India is undergoing a nutrition transition which boosts the development of overweight and obesity leading to chronic diseases such as type 2 diabetes (cf. Shetty 2002: 175/181, Chacko 2003: 1087f., Gujral 2015: 5). Due to industrialisation and modernization, the diet of Indians living in urbanised areas changes from traditional diets to excessive intake of western fast food (cf. Shetty 2002: 177f./181). Besides these dietary factors the rising lack of physical activity is highly associated with the rising emergence of the aforementioned disease (cf. Shetty 2002: 175/177f., Lawton et al. 2006: 44). According to the *Asian Diabetes Prevention Initiative* (website, "Facts and Figures"), in the year 2013 60% of diabetics lived in Asia, whereby India was home to the second largest population of individuals with type 2 diabetes worldwide, with 65.1 million diabetics. In contrast, the *American Diabetes Association* (website, "Statistics About Diabetes") reported 21.9 million diabetics for the year 2012. As a result, the awareness of influencing factors for the development respectively prevention of type 2 diabetes should be quite high for both countries, and even higher for the Asian Indian population. To see if this is the case, in this paper I am going to examine the English language of both cultures with the help of corpus-linguistic analysis.

1.1. Main risk factors for developing Type 2 Diabetes

Some factors influencing the emergence of type 2 diabetes were already mentioned before. Overweight and obesity are clearly the main risk factors for developing type 2 diabetes (cf. Gujral 2015: 5). Asian Indians have a higher percentage of abdominal body fat compared to Europeans, which leads to a higher insulin resistance associated with type 2 diabetes (cf. *Asian Diabetes Prevention Initiative* (website, "Why are Asians at Higher Risk?")). Therefore, Asian Indians have a higher prevalence for developing type 2 diabetes than other ethnic groups, even at a lower Body Mass Index (BMI[1]) (cf. Gujral 2015: 5, Shetty 2002: 178, Chacko 2003: 1087f., Lawton et. al. 2006: 44). Of course, body weight is highly dependent on nutritional factors (cf. Gujral 2015: 5). In addition to the traditional consumption of already unhealthy white rice, refined grains and saturated fats from

---

[1] The BMI is defined by the World Health Organization: Normal weight is classified as BMI 18.5–24.99 kg/m², overweight is classified as BMI 25–29.99 kg/m², and obese is classified as BMI ≥ 30 kg/m².

palm oil, especially the increased consumption of western fast food raises the intake of fat, sugar and calories (cf. *Asian Diabetes Prevention Initiative* (website, "Why are Asians at Higher Risk?")). Furthermore, the rising lack of daily physical activity in Asian Indians promotes the emergence of overweight, obesity and lastly type 2 diabetes (cf. *Asian Diabetes Prevention Initiative* (Ibid.)).

1.2. Awareness of influencing factors for developing and preventing Type 2 Diabetes

The awareness of influencing factors can help Asian Indians to prevent themselves from gaining type 2 diabetes. Affected Individuals can improve or even cure their disease by applying this knowledge to their everyday lifestyle. Murugesan et al. (cf. 2007: 434f.) show that the awareness of influencing factors of diabetes among Asian Indians is generally low. At a total score of 65 – which would reflect a high awareness – 50% of the participants scored below 15 points. Participants were examined for their knowledge of various factors associated with diabetes – such as causes, symptoms and complications, physical activity, unhealthy body size and shape, healthy and unhealthy food and so on. Especially, participants knew very little about the importance of physical activity and healthy diets for preventing and improving type 2 diabetes (cf. 2007: 434f.). By many, overweight and obesity were not seen as risk factors for provoking type 2 diabetes (cf. 2007: 436).

1.3. Awareness and use of alternative medicine for treating Diabetes

I want to take a closer look at the awareness and use of alternative treatments for type 2 diabetes. Since India has a long tradition of ayurvedic medicine, one could assume that Asian Indians have a better knowledge of herbal medicine and other alternative treatments compared to the U.S. Americans for instance. Kumar et al. (cf. 2006: 705) show that the awareness and use of alternative medicine among Indian diabetics was high.[2] In comparison, in the USA only about 40% of the population use alternative medicine (cf. 2006: 706).

---

[2] 71% of the diabetic participants showed awareness of alternative medicine and treatments, from which 67.7% actually used these methods.

2. Leading question and presumptions

Cultural beliefs can affect the perception of various aspects of everyday life, even the mindset towards a disease like type 2 diabetes:

> "Culture (…) is a complex system in which traditions, attitudes, beliefs, and values are acquired, shared and held by a group of people. It affects every aspect of people's lives, including their attitudes toward illness, health status and health-related behaviours." (Chacko 2003: 1088)

Cultural beliefs and attitudes reflect on the language of any society, which can then be seen as a mirror for the awareness of a concept, even medical conditions like diabetes (cf. Geeraerts 2003: 2). In this paper, the Indian and U.S. American cultural model (cf. 2003: 2ff.) of type 2 diabetes will be described through a corpus-linguistic analysis of the two English varieties. In particular, I want to examine the general awareness of type 2 diabetes and its correlating factors among the Asian Indian culture in comparison to the USA. Furthermore, I want to check, whether the Indian English shows a higher awareness for alternative treatments due to the ayurvedic background.

It could be assumed, that Asian Indians have an even higher awareness for the causes of type 2 diabetes than the U.S. population, since Asian Indians are known to have a genetically high prevalence. It could also be assumed, that the Asian Indian culture shows an increased awareness of alternative treatment due to its traditional ayurvedic knowledge.

3. Method and corpus

For reviewing my own assumptions, which are also based on the theoretical background I gave in the Introduction, I will make use of the corpus-linguistic method to examine the Indian English variety and compare the findings with the U.S. English. The Corpus of Global Web-Based English, or short GloWbE, includes 1.9 billion words from web pages in twenty countries speaking different English varieties.[3] It allows the examination of different linguistic information in each of these variations, such as the frequency and use of words, synonyms, grammatical constructions and collocates. Furthermore, it is possible to compare a specific linguistic feature in two selected varieties, e.g. the Indian English and the U.S. English. In the GloWbE -Corpus the U.S. English has a total number of 386,809,355

---

[3] Introductory facts on the GloWbE -Corpus can be found on: http://corpus.byu.edu/glowbe/ .

words. The corpus of the Indian English is 4 times as small as the U.S. English corpus, with only 96,430,888 words. This fact has to be kept in mind in while analysing the output of the search requests.

4. Approach and results

At first I am going to take a look at the general awareness of type 2 diabetes and additionally overweight/obesity in both English varieties. Furthermore, I will examine the correlation between these two aspects, to get an idea of the extent of awareness of overweight/obesity being a causing factor for type 2 diabetes. In the last part I want to check the awareness of different kinds of treatments associated with the disease, such as special diets, exercise and lastly alternative, i.e. ayurvedic, herbal medicine.

4.1. Frequency of Type 2 Diabetes in Indian English and U.S. English

When searching for the keyword "type 2 diabetes" in the GloWbE –Corpus the U.S. English shows a seven to eight times higher total frequency of the token (USA: 812 - India: 119):

SECTION	ALL	US	CA	GB	IE	AU	NZ	IN
FREQ	3364	812	278	762	186	329	267	119
PER MIL	1.79	2.10	2.06	1.97	1.84	2.22	3.28	1.23

Fig. 1: Excerpt from the frequency chart for the word "type 2 diabetes"

But in relation to the total number of words in each variety[4], the absolute frequency in Indian English is above half of the U.S. frequency of tokens (USA: 0,00021% - India: 0,00012%). This seems to reflect the awareness of the rising prevalence of type 2 diabetes in India. But still, the numbers for both English varieties are very low in general.

---

[4] Remember that the Indian English corpus is four times as small as the U.S. English corpus. Therefore the total number of tokens has to be divided by the total number of words in each corpus.

4.2. Frequency of overweight and obesity

The next step is to see how high the awareness of overweight respectively obesity is, as isolated factors which yet are highly associated as a cause of type 2 diabetes. The number of tokens for the keyword "overweight" lies at 3328 for the U.S. English and 659 for the Indian English. This results in an absolute frequency of 0,00086% for the U.S. English and 0,00068% for the Indian English. Hence, the general awareness of overweight in the Asian Indian population is nearly as high as in the USA:

SECTION	ALL	US	CA	GB	IE	AU	NZ	IN
FREQ	14207	3328	1059	3043	842	1632	716	659
PER MIL	7.54	8.60	7.86	7.85	8.33	11.01	8.80	6.83

Fig. 2: Excerpt from the frequency chart for the word "overweight"

Obesity, which is an excessive form of overweight and an even larger risk factor for developing type 2 diabetes shows a slightly increased number of tokens. With 5190 entries the U.S. English corpus shows an absolute frequency of 0,00134%, India has an absolute frequency of 0,00095% with a total number of 912 tokens. The general awareness of obesity in India is again nearly as high as in the USA:

SECTION	ALL	US	CA	GB	IE	AU	NZ	IN
FREQ	19180	5190	1824	3767	916	2220	868	912
PER MIL	10.18	13.42	13.53	9.72	9.07	14.98	10.66	9.46

Fig. 3: Excerpt from the frequency chart for the word "obesity"

In summary it can be said, that the awareness of overweight and obesity is again very low, as it was before with the general awareness of type 2 diabetes.

4.3. Type 2 Diabetes and its correlation with overweight and obesity

To see, if there is a higher awareness for overweight and obesity being a risk factor for type 2 diabetes it is necessary to request GloWbE for the correlation between these aspects. I searched for the collocations "type 2 diabetes" – "over-weight/obesity" which would be possible to be detected in the corpus up to nine words to the left and to the right of the keyword. For the U.S. English I received 21 entries and only 3 for the Indian English for the collocation with the term "overweight". The collocation with "obesity" gave me 73 results for the U.S. English and only 8 for the Indian English. Both frequencies show a generally low awareness of overweight respectively obesity being amplifying factors for type 2 diabetes in both cultures, but even more in the Indian culture.

A demonstration of the use of these collocations and the understanding of the correlation of the mentioned aspects in each English variety is given below:

1) U.S. -English:
   "Being overweight does increase your risk for developing type 2 diabetes, and a diet high in calories from any source contributes to weight gain."[5]

2) Asian Indian English:
   "The major chunk of Indian population suffering from this disease has Type 2 diabetes which is closely associated with obesity and consumption of junk and fast foods especially in metropolitan cities", discloses Dr. Bhambani at Mool-chand.[6]

These two examples already illustrate the awareness of the effect that an unhealthy diet has on gaining weight, which is a risk factor for developing type 2 diabetes. The assumed to be Indian doctor in the second example further implicates, that this trend could be ascribed to the modernization and industrialization of the Indian culture.

4.4. Awareness of different forms of treatment for Type 2 Diabetes

The main treatments for type 2 diabetes are known to be regular exercise, a healthy diet and if needed medicinal therapy (cf. Lawton 2006: 43, Chacko 2003: 1088). Alternative, i.e. herbal practice, can additionally be used for relieve of symptoms of the disease. To get some insight into the general awareness of treatments for type 2 diabetes I searched for the collocation "type 2 diabetes" – "treatment". I received 19 results in the U.S. English corpus and only 3 for the Indian English. This first general request gave an impression on the use of herbal medicine in India, since the collocations "alternative", "ayurvedic", "herbal" and "plants" with the keyword "type 2 diabetes" gave absolutely no result for the In-

---

[5] Source: http://www.diabetes.org/diabetes-basics/diabetes-myths/
[6] Source: http://zeenews.india.com/exclusive/india-in-race-with-china-to-become-global-diabetic-capital_5848.html

dian English. The following example for the Indian English can be seen as a representative for the ayurvedic medicine in the Indian culture:

3) *"[Cinnamon] helps control blood sugar levels and is very useful in the treatment of type 2 diabetes. You can use a teaspoon of cinnamon with a glass of water, cinnamon tea, cinnamon liquid extract or cinnamon supplement."*[7]

The following, selected example gives us a general impression of the awareness of diabetes therapy in the USA:

4) *"Treatment for type 2 diabetes is first treated with weight reduction, a diabetic diet, and exercise. When these measures fail to control the elevated blood sugar, oral medications are used. If oral medications are still insufficient, insulin medications are considered."*[8]

In the U.S. American culture diet and exercise are taken as essential elements for treating and monitoring diabetes. Medicinal treatments are only used if necessary. But there is some evidence for the use of alternative treatments in the USA. The collocation "type 2 diabetes" – "alternative" resulted in 2 entries from the U.S. English corpus:

5) *"Xagave is a low GI [Glycemic Index] sweetener which makes it good for people already diagnosed with type 2 Diabetes as well as a good alternative for those who want to avoid it."*[9]

"Xagave" is syrup made from the agave plant, which can be used in a diet low on highly glycemic food which can increase the blood sugar level. This example represents the awareness of the use of special plants for treating type 2 diabetes. It also reflects the high awareness of various diabetes diets in the USA, since the collocation "type 2 diabetes" – "diet" gave me 34 results for the U.S. English and only 5 entries for the Indian English. Besides the "Low GI diet" various other diets can be found in association with type 2 diabetes, such as the "Low carb diet" or "Low fat diet", the "Vegan diet", the "Paleo(lithic) diet" and the "Mediterranean diet:

6) U.S. English:
"Choosing vegetable sources of fat and protein may also lower your risk of heart disease and type 2 diabetes. Mediterranean-style diets may be effective."[10]

In comparison to the USA the Indian culture seems to have a low awareness of the use of diabetes diets in general, since the collocation "type 2 diabetes" – "diet"

---

[7] Source: http://expertscolumn.com/content/7-spices-long-and-healthy-life

[8] Source: http://www.medicinenet.com/dyspepsia/page4.htm

[9] Source: http://www.xagave.com/learn/5-infographics-sugar-ignore/

[10] Source: http://www.hsph.harvard.edu/nutritionsource/healthy-weight/healthy-weight-full-story/

resulted in only 5 entries. An example for the understanding of the use of a healthy diet is given below:

> 7) *"[T]ype 2 Diabetes is usually caused by the way a particular person lives their life. By following a stringent diet and presenting regular exercise you can greatly help prevent this form of Diabetes."*[11]

In the examples 4) and 7) we could already see the awareness of exercising as a way of treatment in both cultures. When searching for the specific collocation "type 2 diabetes" – "exercise" I got 14 tokens for The U.S. English and no results for the Indian English. The following example from the U.S. English corpus summarizes the understanding of the importance of a healthy nutrition and regular exercise in the therapy of type 2 diabetes:

> 8) *"It is my contention that health care providers, including physicians, nurse prac-titioners, and diabetes educators, need to impress upon their patients with Type 2 diabetes that getting regular, almost daily exercise is equally as important as watching what they eat."*[12]

In summary it can be said, that the U.S. English corpus reflects a higher awareness of diabetes treatments in comparison to the Indian English corpus, es-pecially concerning dietetic and physical therapy. Furthermore, the USA has an especially broad knowledge of various kinds of diets. The use of herbal medicine could not be displayed in both English varieties, which was unlikely for the Indian culture and its ayurvedic tradition.

5. Summary and discussion

Although the U.S. and the Indian English displays a high awareness for over-weight and obesity in general, their correlation with type 2 diabetes seems to be little known in both cultures, but even less in India. Furthermore, the Indian Eng-lish shows a low awareness for diabetic-specific treatments in general, i.e. healthy diets and exercise. These findings reflect the preceded groundwork in paragraph 1.2 „Awareness of influencing factors for developing and preventing Type 2 Dia-betes" (p. 2). Here, it was reported that the awareness of influencing factors of diabetes among Asian Indians is generally low. In addition, the presumption that the Indian culture would show an increased use of alternative (i.e. ayurvedic, herbal) medicine, could not be confirmed in the analysis of the Indian English

---

[11] Source: http://www.myarticlestory.com/free-diabetic-guidelines-information-for-anyone-suffering-from-diabetes
[12] Source: http://www.huffingtonpost.com/milt-bedingfield/diabetes-exercise_b_1553833.html

corpus. Whereas Chacko (2002: 1087) reports that "[Asian Indians] (...) frequently used Ayurvedic medicine and folk herbal remedies as supplements." However, due to Kumar et al. (cf. 2006: 708/710f., see also Chacko 2003: 1088) the awareness and use of ayurvedic medicine is in fact associated with a higher education and higher socio-economic rank. Hence, the knowledge and use of herbs and medicinal plants is not mainly restricted to poor and uneducated individuals, as assumed due to their lower expense. Altogether, Murugesan et al. (cf. 2007: 433ff.) ascertained that higher education and professional or executive job positions correlate heavily with better awareness. Furthermore, individuals with diabetes had better knowledge than the general population. Another factor that might explain the lower awareness in the Indian population is a lesser access to health care (cf. Gujral 2015:5f., Chacko 2003: 1088). As Murugesan et al. (2007: 436) state:

> "Creating an awareness about the disease, its causes, treatment and complications is the first step in the crusade against this disease. Several countries like India which have a large burden of diabetes lack a structured national programme for creating an awareness about the disease."

The outcome of the corpus-linguistic analysis of the two English varieties represents the cultural approach towards a chronic disease like type 2 diabetes. Especially in India socio-economic aspects, including general health education, play a large role regarding the awareness of the disease and its influencing factors: "[E]xperiences of [type 2 diabetes] and (...) health management decisions are closely linked to [the] cultural background and the environmental resources of the region" (Chacko 2002: 1087).

6. References

American Diabetes Association. *Statistics About Diabetes* (18th May 2015). Retrieved from http://www.diabetes.org/diabetes-basics/statistics/ (access on 15th June 2015).

Asian Diabetes Prevention Initiative. *Facts and Figures* (n.d.). Retrieved from http://asiandiabetesprevention.org/what-is-diabetes/facts-and-figures (access on 15th June 2015).

Asian Diabetes Prevention Initiative. *Why are Asians at Higher Risk?* (n.d.). Retrieved from http://asiandiabetesprevention.org/what-is-diabetes/why-are-asians-higher-risk (access on 15th June 2015).

Chacko, Elizabeth (2002). Culture and therapy: complementary strategies for the treatment of type-2 diabetes in an urban setting in Kerala, India. In: *Social Science and Medicine* 56, 1087-1098. Retrieved from https://www.researchgate.net/publication/10893788_Culture_and_therapy_complementary_strategies_for_the_treatment_of_type-2_diabetes_in_an_urban_setting_in_Kerala_India (access on 12th June 2015).

Geeraerts, Dirk. 2003. Cultural models of linguistic standardization. In: Dirven, René/Frank, Roslyn/Pütz, Martin (eds.). Cognitive Models in Language and Thought. Ideology, Metaphors and Meanings. Berlin: Mouton de Gruyter, 25-68. Retrieved from http://wwwling.arts.kuleuven.be/qlvl/PDFPublications/03Culturalmodels.pdf (access on 12th June 2015).

Gujral, Unjali P. et. al. (2015). Comparing Type 2 Diabetes, Prediabetes, and Their Associated Risk Factors in Asian Indians in India and in the U.S.: The CARRS and MASALA Studies. In: *Diabetes Care* Vol. 38, 4, 1-7. Retrieved from https://www.researchgate.net/publication/275053332_Comparing_Type_2_Diabetes_Prediabetes_and_Their_Associated_Risk_Factors_in_Asian_Indians_in_India_and_in_the_U.S._The_CARRS_and_MASALA_Studies (access on 12th June 2015).

Kumar, D./Bajaj, S./Mehrotra, R. (2006). Knowledge, attitude and practice of complementary and alternative medicines for diabetes. In: *Public Health* 120, 705–711. Retrieved from https://www.researchgate.net/profile/Ravi_Mehrotra/publication/6957504_Knowledge_attitude_and_practice_of_complementary_and_alternative_medicines_for_diabetes/links/0deec52c1081ababaf000000.pdf (access on 13th June 2015).

Lawton, J. et. al. (2006). 'I can't do any serious exercise': barriers to physical activity amongst people of Pakistani and Indian origin with Type 2 diabetes. In: *Health Education Research* 21, 1, 43-54. Retrieved from http://her.oxfordjournals.org/content/21/1/43.full.pdf+html (acces on 12th June 2015).

Murugesan, N. et al. (2007). Awareness about diabetes and its complications in the general and diabetic population in a city in southern India. In: *Diabetes Research and Clinical Practice* 77, 433–437. Retrieved from https://www.researchgate.net/profile/Snehalatha_Chamukuttan/publication/6512827_Awareness_about_diabetes_and_its_complications_in_the_general_and_diabetic_population_in_a_city_in_southern_India/links/00b49529042eccbf82000000.pdf (access on 12th June 2015).

Shetty, Prakash S. (2002). Nutrition transition in India. In: *Public Health Nutrition* 5, 1A, 175-182. Retrieved from http://journals.cambridge.org/download.php?file=%2FPHN%2FPHN5_1a%2FS1368980002000253a.pdf&code=7a2e141dff91f07413924f0d065b8fde (access on 15th June 2015).

Corpus
http://corpus.byu.edu/glowbe/